BIG MONEY PORNO MOMMY

Big Money Porno Mommy

Cover design and layout by Catherine Weiss.

Edited by Ally Ang and Josh Savory.

www.gameoverbooks.com

BIG MONEY PORNO MOMMY

POEMS

CATHERINE WEISS

For my mom, who isn't supposed to be reading this one

CONTENTS

"I know writers who use subtext and they're all cowards."

GARTH MARENGHI'S DARKPLACE

BIG MONEY PORNO MOMMY

i'm worrying about my body while looking in the opposite direction

my third-grade teacher calls my parents
to claim my constant eye rolling disrespects her
she doesn't guess the scratchy pressure building
until i send my gaze to the speckled ceiling for relief
has only to do with the rotten hollow i feel growing in my center
      like a scooped pumpkin left molding in the sun

suddenly i am made entirely of armpits and breasts
i don't know about sex yet but i have formed the question not to ask
      i hear the word *blossom* a lot
i'm dreading the world's hunger and hoping to be found tasty

muscles in my throat pull back and sideways
      i don't know about anxiety yet
only that the days are stretched and if you pluck a too-tight string
      it will snap

i've tucked taut the sheets on my twin bed
the things children won't admit to wanting could fill an ocean

grown-ups are making lists naming
      the *perfectly normal developments*
but it's all pubic hair and maxi pads
nothing about being eaten by giant dog-men
      nothing about whatever a child thinks fucking is

when my eyes roll up
      it's like pouring water on a screaming hot skillet
        all i see is steam

IDAHO

we adopted the rottweiler
from the pound and named her
idaho   she was a nice family pet
except for barking at
then attacking any two
people attempting to touch

in private I would run
my finger along the channels
of her fur   honor her
nervous jaw and the dabs
of tan above her eyes

just a kid attempting some self-
conscious gesture towards healing

this is how I will show idaho
I love her this is how she learns
she is good   for ten years
in our house we didn't embrace

said a dog was the reason why

CUTTING CARDS

there, in the shag-carpeted room
above the garage,
drunk on warm sprite
and the promise of thirteen,
we agree to play strip poker
with the boys.

they outnumber us 2 to 1.
this statistic plants sea-urchins
in the tide pool of my belly,
each what-if bursting
with prickly, alien anticipation.

we agree to play as a team—
i refuse to strip
& Grace doesn't know the rules,
so i become the brain;
she becomes the body.
this is the dichotomy of girl-hood,
the familiar parsing
of ourselves to earn
a seat at the table.

i am still hazy
on the distinction
of being wanted vs. welcomed.
i do not yet know
where i fit;
who i should pretend to be.

as the game grinds on,
the boys grow bashful,
avert their eyes from Grace
& her underwear.

i diligently study the flop,
the turn, the river,
but all attention in the room
is focusing, blue-hot & brittle,
two inches above
Grace's belly button.

she crosses her freckled arms
& i don't look at her face.
there's something here
i want for myself:
to press a finger pad
to this stovetop surface.

this is the moment i decide
i too must yield
my layers until i am the one thing
in the room
so desirable
everyone knows
to look away.

THE PHONE SEX POEM

i never did it as a job
it was more like my unpaid internship

in high school i had a boyfriend who loved phone sex

the performance took an hour every day
i said sexy stuff into a landline
and he masturbated very slowly
(it was rude the pace he masturbated)

it wasn't terrible in the beginning

he used his words:
>   *i need it*
>   *don't you love me?*
>   *give me a little relief*
>   *no one can do it like you can*
>   *if you hang up i will kill myself*

every day for three years

turns out i'll say a lot of shit to get somebody off
the phone

i'll talk about cuckolding, watersports, incest
hell i'll pretend to fuck an errant lobsterman
i'll tell you i crawled naked into the woods to take a shit like a dog
this is a fact i know about myself
i will say literally anything
with my back against a wall

CATHERINE AND I, (SUMMER '00)

i've been afraid of flying since 9/11 or maybe it was the summer i cut off all my hair without asking permission. he kept a photo of me on his website. his trophy in yellow. these days i cancel cross-country travel & spend my nights checking up on the locks. caption looks like: *nose-dive.* at some point i stop hoping the plane pulls up. at some point i'm just waiting for someone else to happen.

IN THE VIRAL VIDEO

I was wearing my best clothes.
The first comment says
I must've been desperate for attention,
doing a trauma poem.

The first comment says
I'm too fat to be
doing a trauma poem
in a see-through shirt.

I'm too fat to be
showing up on stage
in a see-through shirt,
wanting to feel something good.

I showed up on stage
trying to say what happened.
I wanted to feel something good,
I didn't know better.

I'm trying to say what happened.
I was thirteen,
I didn't know better
when I met him.

I was thirteen—
I must've been desperate for attention.
When I met him
I was wearing my best clothes.

HOW TO LIKE IT

There's something to be said, I suppose, for the perfunctory
jackhammering of mainstream pornography, the accepted
range of high-pitched vocalizations, its overall clinical hairlessness.
Pornography has reorganized my brain, taught me what to like
and how to like it. Women, the ones I count favorites, are young,
agreeable, and pretending. I wonder if watching them means
I would like to be fucking the most vulnerable version of myself—
if I'm jealous of the men who got to me first or maybe I'm trying
to find the piece that was slipped off at the bedside, crumpled
to the floorboards, and never picked up again. Porn taught me early
to shape my desires around boys, like an arm hugs a body, or rather,
like a mouth takes a cock. We don't talk about how porn births
a need for itself. I don't know if I could return to the wild
pathways of my wandering mind. I'd like to try. Imagine two people
who've longed for each other ten years, three months, and 17 days
finally acknowledge their mutual hunger. Watch them shyly undress
together for the first time, naked bodies glowing in the misty-blue
predawn daylight. They're saying yes yes yes. So am I.

THE PHONE SEX POEM

there's someone breathing / somewhere / someone is feeling desire / the rush of wanting something he's not supposed to / and receiving it / i am giving him the thing he wants / i am the thing / the fantasy / it is me and also not-me / an approximation of hot / i am a sex toy / an actress / a believable unbelievability / it doesn't matter what he believes / as long as he cums / this is a battle of wills / of what i will stoop to say to reclaim some hours of freedom / he goes for long minutes without even touching his erection / i can tell / he wants me to know we're on his schedule / he wants as much of the drug as he can get / my kink is goodbye / my kink is hanging up the phone / my kink is his reluctant quivering moan / my kink is vocalizing through my geometry homework / because i have actual important things to attend to / and this is just another task / i'm learning: men are great / before they come to need your gifts / how can i expect to be an object of desire / and not also a receptacle / i try not to watch the clock / i try to keep it secret from my roommate / this dirty / place i go / what am i good for / who am i good for / or to / the thing i love about men is how well i can play their game / it's pretty simple / say a few words: / i want you to fuck me / i think about it every day / how much i want your hard / cock / cock hard / cock / wet dirty / cock / hole / cock in hole / wet cum / sweet / hot sweet cum cock in hole / etc // real sex is very quiet / quieter than i would actually prefer / but i don't want to get caught in someone else's fantasy / because somewhere / breathing / he remembers what i said / and he likes it

BEFORE THE APPS, THERE WAS CRAIGSLIST

i'm 19, lonely,
and so far believe
i'm straight.
i occasionally
toss a late-night post
on the craigslist
personals,
because such a thing
still exists.
it's secret but
i get hundreds
of responses
before the morning
sends me
scurrying back to
intermediate french,
classical mythology.
witty men. dull men.
handsome and homely men.
ingratiating men.
cocky men.
all of them bored,
unhappy men.
sometimes a thousand
or more in one go.
it's too easy.
men like 19. i like
email. everybody wins.

EKPHRASIS OF "BOWLING ALLEY
GANGBANG - BUKAKI [sic] ENDING"

The back room is depressing, its low ceiling just beams
and fiberglass insulation the color of brains.
Machinery. Harsh lighting.
Then, a barrage of average dicks—unrelenting swarms
like Hitchcock's The Birds.
The woman seems to be having a nice time, thank god.
Some of the men wear masks.
I watch pornography twice a week
but I am more haunted by BOWLING ALLEY GANGBANG
than by that two-headed calf poem,
goosebumps beyond Good Bones.
You could make this bowling alley beautiful.
What does it mean to watch? I don't want to
want to. I'm fascinated by what art could be
and isn't. If we meet in a frenzy,
take it seriously. Bowling is in decline.
There are still twelve thousand bowling alleys in the world.
I always wanted to be useful, too.

MENACE

once i let a roommate i hardly knew lead me
into midnight forest beyond a freeway exit ramp.

he said there was a swimming hole. i watched him
hold his beer like a fucked-up bird

and i said why not. i don't know if he carried
that night but when i tell this story

i picture his handgun nestled in a waistband
wide awake. mouthing o you stupid bitch.

there is a calculation. maybe you know it.
go along in your right fist, *enough* in your left.

now i know not to walk into the woods
with drunk men who hate me. but i knew then, too.

the future as a kitchen with the lights turned off.
the past, every riverbed that didn't kill you.

THE PHONE SEX POEM

i am into: porn. hair pulling. some rough play. butts. necks. arms. hairiness. hairlessness. slow sex. hard sex. sex-sex. sex-without-sex. tension. watching. teeth. tongues. suction. powerlessness in the hands of someone i trust. vice versa. sensory overwhelm. talking about sex. writing about sex. thinking and thinking and thinking about sex.

i am not into: poop. infantilization. family. people who don't want me.

the point of all the phone sex i had in my teens seemed to be finding the things i wasn't hot for and making me enact them. the point was to make me. the point was his power. my acquiescence.

after years of doing what i didn't want, i shut the window and closed the blinds with finality. i don't know if it's possible to pry it open without breaking something.

i want a playground. i want a piece of graph paper. i want to doodle. design. i want to build a monument to all the things that take me: the way i curl into myself when i cum. the insistence of desire. the queering of power dynamics. the weight of another body. the weight of my body. the negotiation of it. the fumbling. the satisfaction. the alchemy that turns watching The Fifth Element on a dorm room bed into something human and naked and wanted.

ALL MY FRIENDS ARE FROM PORNHUB

i placed nausea bands around my wrists
hard plastic clits pressed between tendons

pressure is a gradual prayer
i try anything to keep lunch down

my gut full of crumbling coals
an unpregnant uncertain whimpering mess

the only thing i know helps every time
is to go to bed and find relief

just like dorothy i wake up to friends
you were there and you and you and you—

TO HELL WITH BOYS WHO PLAY ACOUSTIC GUITAR

i keep more rage in my shoulders than i actually recall his specifics.

or maybe all the things he prevented me from doing are now realer

than the time i spent enduring him. after i left, he wrote me

into the album. charming boy loved the wrong girl. fine then,

i'll be your shrieking kettle. on and on and on and on. satellite.

echo. killer lyric for the bridge. i wish i could unclench my fists.

DISSOCIATIVE EPISODE AS GAUSSIAN BLUR

[illegible]

[illegible]

[illegible]

[illegible] all day long to stay upright

time must still be passing but

i've been elsewhere for four days

the snow falls on indifferent pines

my reflection in the window again

[illegible]

[illegible]

[illegible]

BULLY

when my husband says it's because
i'm a good person that i let you in again
i want to tell him he doesn't understand me

like you do. all the monsters under my bed
are just men doing their best.
i can sense your disappointment.

your life is shitty but so is your letter to the editor.
no, you can't reject a rejection.
there is no story of us. i know you

loved to hurt me. i can see you're still trying.
maybe you're right. maybe once
our sorrows touched elbows.

but i'm better now. happier than you—you,
moth caught in a rainstorm, instrument
of misery. i don't want to know you anymore

because you're mean, soft-mean.
a loud cat in an empty house, the obvious twist
to a book i've long since put down.

ALONE TIME

legs, tits, and butts, rhythmically smacking
sort of like a band (but mostly like porn)
there is music and we are dancing
like we've got an orchestra behind us
only here, the cellos are dicks and the
timpani are dicks and the piccolos
are smaller dicks and the conductor is
some guy with a production company

you are the marqueed name, prima donna—
my body hurts a little bit less now
and i want to say thank you for waltzing
or doing the job few people respect
or letting me press myself to myself,
picking it up and then putting it down

ADULT • CHRISTIAN • DEATH • FAMILY • FRIENDSHIP •
HAIKU • HOPE • HUMOR • LGBTQ • LOVE • NATURE •
PAIN • RHYME • SAD • SOCIETY • SPIRITUAL • TEEN

the *browse category* sidebar on popular poem sharing
website AllPoetry.com reminds me of pornhub,
unfortunately. just picture the videos.

what is a haiku porn like? seventeen
pelvic thrusts. no more and no less.
and how might the erotic rhyme?

some categories make me laugh. some don't.
death pornography exists but shouldn't.
society porn spills sloppily from screens

around the world. more hope porn, please.
and sad porn, but intentionally sad porn only:
one final hurrah porn, catharsis porn,

nostalgia porn. now i'm imagining entirely new
genres of dirty video. don't you want to play
this game, exchange these lovers' sweatshirts?

the words are even similar. poem. porn.
puckering my lips is not coincidence.
if you don't like porn or poems then i think

you haven't found a type that whispers to you.
the collaboration goes both ways. hear me out.
an explicit poem. a dp poem. the poem's

bleached and hairless asshole. you know what
i mean when i say i want to read verse that fucks.
go ahead, write a poem that licks my teeth.

i can't picture what kind of dirty talk i would even enjoy receiving. mostly the things i think about are quiet. a musky shirt-collar. prolonged eye contact. a belligerent smile. repressing laughter. sex as a joke i can't stop laughing at.

i think about taking something that wants to be taken. i think about leaving a party with my husband. saying goodbye to absolutely no one, including the host. i think about undressing in a hallway. i think about a belt. i think about taking my time with said belt. i think about each notch slipping under the buckle, becoming opened and also undone. good sex is wanted sex, of course. but good sex might not be clean. i want to be unclean without feeling like spoiled fruit. i want to be consumed without disappearing.

it's complicated, this dancing. sometimes i want to be convinced. sometimes it's a game. sometimes to be won is winning. sometimes i want to be pushed. to let someone push you is an opportunity to be brave. sometimes i want to be put on a pedestal. sometimes i want to be down on the floor.

SUCKING AND FUCKING

i only cry at the profound.
the two parts sorrow, one part hope.
i drink that milk like i've never
been more thirsty for anything.
like this time it might quench
a deeper part of my cracking gut.
how do you believe in love?
i am, myself, a creep. power-hungry.
people generally like me, and yet
the truth is i wish i had a dick so that
i could find somebody to suck it.
and i'm nice person. just imagine.
but when no one puts an eye
to my cage, i rattle these bars, i do.
nature is the wildest yowling barncat.
feral, in heat, and spitting pissed.
left alone, i might eat my young
and weep over their shortened stories.
how pretty. but this landscape,
we make of it lace. that is my impulse,
too. i like to scrunch my face into a wet
broken mask. you also. i see it
between your lines. the sweetness of flight,
the lie. the half-belief. and the turning.

REWARD GOOD BEHAVIOR AND IGNORE THEM WHEN THEY'RE NAUGHTY

aubade for the man who DMed me good morning
after messaging me the night before to correct my spelling
of *bukakke*. aubade for the man who stopped me
in the middle of a bout at the national poetry slam
to tell me about his vintage porno VHS collection.
aubade for all the men, everywhere, in general.
a poem is not an invitation unless it is. a poem begs
to be seen and never touched unless it does. my therapist
asked why i'm not excited when a man wants to talk to me.
maybe he is nothing until he does something i want.

GOOD FUNDAMENTALS

The relationship was curdling, and we both could taste it.
I hated sports on principle, but he was a Knicks fan

so I brought him to a late-season game to demonstrate how quick
a person can change. April 25, 2012. Knicks vs Clippers.

I took him to dinner. I got great seats. I held that night
like my last lit match, breathless. One chance to be dynamic,

a fun girlfriend who surprises her lover with basketball tickets,
nights on the town, shared interests. Laid it all on the line.

If the Knicks win, I bargained, he'll be happy enough
to love me again. The Knicks didn't lose. We lasted a week,

maybe two. Much can hinge on a moment of extreme pressure,
or maybe it just looks that way. But a person can change,

though it took me ten years to love basketball and these days
I root for the Celtics. Tonight they're embarrassing the Hornets,

up almost 40 points, and I'm learning what it feels like
to be crushing it. My father texts me to say he saw an interview

with Luke Kornet, our new center, in which he was asked,
How do you stay ready to play after sitting game after game?

If I had it to do again, I'd still buy the Knicks tickets,
pin my hopes to a team I cared nothing for. Kornet answered,

It's hard for all the guys, but no matter how I feel I'm still 7'2".

FOLD

sometimes i look at old pictures of myself   with the shiny
        hair & décolletage & inoffensive little tummy & say yeah
i bet she liked to fuck   as though i hadn't also been there
        the whole time   making habit of slithering from
my skin   & faking all those unearned orgasms for men
        who certainly deserved no such consideration   & wanting
lovers who wanted me back   but then having to contend
        with the humanness of the imperfect screw   & subsequent
morning after   & fretting about who was possibly going to walk in
        & yell *you can do it but not like that freak* & i think it's true
i've always needed to pretend   i didn't have a body
        to love another person's body   or maybe it's more
i might've had a body   but was only borrowing her   temporarily
        & shortly would be upgrading to a newer model
& most days now i feel too smelly   to be having sex anyway
        because the fat   & the rolls of my belly legs back & arms
have folds   which often after showering don't adequately dry
        even when toweled thoroughly   which is difficult
& i'm usually exhausted even at the prospect of trying to get clean
        & sometimes i   mammal that i am   get sweaty anyway
& bacteria flourishes   a thick slick in the pits of my flesh
        becoming red & hot & angry   & in those times
when i am in the most shame & pain   the part of me that still desires
        any touch at all   feels like she is almost   all the way
gone

THE PHONE SEX POEM

talking about sex is fascinating / talking about sex is a striptease where nakedness may or may not be the endgame / but it is always in the room / or at least / it's always in the room / for me / and to be sure / i don't want to fuck everyone i meet / but every body has a smell / and every smell is talking to my hindbrain / and not everybody i talk to / do i talk to about sex / i think phone sex is just a caricature of talking about sex / but talking about sex is like / foreplay, maybe, plus mutual masturbation / phone sex / or / dirty talk / is like how i watch the nastiest porn right before i cum / the stuff i have to turn off immediately afterwards / embarrassment flushing out of me like tears / mindless escalation / the warping of wanting / talking about sex is rarely pure academics / some stages are people / some people draw back their curtains for this kind of thing / wholehearted / welcome to my show / talking about sex is like fucking somebody without confronting my own desire to be naked / talking about sex is plausible deniability / talking about sex is safe sex / and also more dangerous than the bodies doing what they tend to do / i do not feel / safe

BIG MONEY PORNO MOMMY

To choose my work; of strong legs; to get married
and stay that way; to make mistakes; to omit;

of social currency; of eating well; of good
health insurance; to never be pregnant; to move

to a different state and then back again; of a loving
family; to insist my desires matter; to speak, walk,

read, create; to try to tell the truth of my life;
to walk through an open door; all of it—power.

MOM FACTS

My mother doesn't respect the breakfast served at her B&B.
My mother thinks fruit brochettes
are bullshit. My mother likes The New Yorker.
My mother loves her garden.
My mother travels once a year
to Switzerland with her husband.
My mother is getting older.
My mother has started shopping for cemetery plots.
Her father died after falling on his sailboat.
Her mother died in balance class at her retirement community.
My mother had *a dismal childhood* with many ugly haircuts.
My mother told me: don't get a dog. She said:
never have children. My mother once called me an elephant.
She says she's been a terrible mother.
I tell her no, she's been good. I say I love you, Mom
when I put her on the Greyhound home.

I ALWAYS USE A STOPWATCH TO TIME MY HIGHS AFTER TAKING EDIBLES

My life, a slideshow. I am certain
I am actually still in college,
taking drugs for the first time,
my whole existence since has been a dream.

Suddenly, I am watching Family Guy,
feeling heat in my face.
My inner monologue going: I'm an animal,
one of a species who feels

shame viscerally. I am contemplating
the concept of inner monologue.
I'm in the bathroom sitting on the floor.
I'm in bed watching the walls collapse.

Time stops completely. I'm shaking.
I'm giving a man I must know
a hug. He is explaining the concept
of getting high. I got too high, he says.

I have no idea what any of this means.
Acceleration. Adrenaline pooling
on the ground around my ankles. I am a poet.
People have parents. Everybody's born.

Everybody dies. I piece together the facts
of this alien life. It seems absurd.
So absurd I must have made it up.
The terror of the thought:

when I come out of this, I will be
a different person. I come out of it
okay, though a little weirded out.
I suspect that reporting on bad trips

is like relating dreams. Less interesting
to everyone else. Regardless,
several nights ago I dreamt I was holding a baby.
The baby wasn't mine.

The baby said to me, "start your timer"
and I said, "I don't have a clock on me"
and the baby looked at me with tiny objective eyes
and whispered, "start your timer *now*."

Then somehow the baby pooped in my mouth.
When my therapist asks me
how I feel about never having children,
I tell her this dream. We laugh.

I don't tell her what happened next,
how the baby turned to rubber and then cloth.
How long I held her in my trembling hands.
How tight I gripped that strip of rag.

THE CERAMIC KNIFE HAS A HANDLE

pale green as pea shoots.
it lives in the utensil drawer in my kitchen.

there are many ways to raise a child. i am not a child.
i remember a dream

about my mother,
that in the room where

she gave birth to me
she raised up that blade, stabbed me four or five times

in the chest, puncturing lung and heart,
and as i lay

on my birthbed gasping
i saw there were tears on my mother's face,

and beyond her sorrow was her anger,
and beyond my mother

was the white sheetrock ceiling and past even our enclosure
were, must have been, stars—

YOU'RE THE ONE WHO HAS TO LEAVE

you're the one at the mall listening to Fastball
on your Hello Kitty minidisc player.
you're the one buying the beads
at the craft store for the perfect choker
to wear to the dance on Friday.
you're the one in the flare jeans
not dancing with Tim in the dark cafeteria
cuz nobody twelve knows how to ask.
you're the one who grows up to throw up
by the side of Rte 15 on the way to work
because of stress. you're the one
with the ugly ponytail. you're getting old
but you're the same person
as you ever were, only less gossip.
not none, but less. you're the one
who once joked to the awkward girl
you were interviewing to be a roommate,
as she lingered in conversation by the door,
you're the one who has to leave.
nobody laughed, except you did, later,
didn't you. don't you still, sometimes,
chuckle at the mean thing you said,
even if you weren't trying to be malicious.
you're the one who felt like a receptacle
for cruelty on the playground,
bus, classroom, gymnasium.
you're the one who calls herself
hypocrite late at night instead of sleeping,
still. still, last night you dreamt of Tim,
who would not dance with you then
but might dance with you now. you're the one
stricken with vestigial longing. before dawn
he whispers something almost gentle.

i could talk about boners all day long if i had to but i think in the grand
scheme of being alive i am done telling men they have made me *wet.*

BUNDLE OF JOY

if you are ever handed a gun
in a social setting

there is this funny
expectation

that you coo
over design or heft,

maybe portability.
it is polite to find

some reason to admire
the machine.

when the new friend
laid the weapon

onto my lap
i couldn't appreciate

in that moment
its promise of violence.

your gun is beautiful.
you should be very proud.

i am thinking of the newborn
my sister-in-law birthed

two days ago.
i'm afraid

for two different reasons
but my hands

feel dangerous
in just one way.

MONEY CHANGES EVERYTHING

i am a bag of snakes so i play cyndi lauper.
my husband tells me i am good
at dancing with a tone that is neither
sarcastic nor indicates i am good at dancing.
i shake my butt. i punch the air. i kick aimlessly,
concerning the dogs.

soon it will be night—
i will sit, write, and eat grilled cheese.
i will think about bills and scribble numbers
on scrap-paper. but first i will flail my limbs
in the kitchen. these joyful movements.
          this thrilling noise.

IN WHICH GOOD WILL HUNTING TELLS ME WHAT MY PROBLEM IS

It's not your favorite flick, and yet you watched it three times this month. It's not your failure to make it as a screenwriter that's disappointing. It's not your faith, as nice as it would be to have it. It's not your fancy party to dress up for on TV. It's not your friends' job to keep the friendships alive. It's not your feast on the table. It's not your fat causing your pain. It's not your fitful and familiar dreams. It's not your fun personality. It's not your family to lose. It's not your future to be frightened of. It's not your face squinching up at the part where Dr. Sean Maguire tells me: *It's not your fault. It's not your fault. Son. It's not your fault.* But. It's not your fuckin' apple, either.

MY MOTHER ASKS IF I FEEL LIKE I'M IN SOMEONE ELSE'S LIFE

i was at brunch on mother's day, she says, *my kids with other moms.*
the easy thing would be to prod. ask her what she regrets,
if it's motherhood. if i'm the one who snatched her rightful life.
i wasn't supposed to be a poet. wasn't supposed to settle

in the town i did, live childless in the 'burbs. require care.
i thought i'd stay in manhattan, live the way you see
on television, by which i mean, working in television.
i've been eating someone else's omelet for a decade.

i tell my mother i think each lifetime contains many lives,
some of them are more ours than others. i say i miss tennis,
am trying to accept i may never play again, i make choices.
okay sure, she replies, *but other people make choices for us, too.*

THE PHONE SEX POEM

i am aware of my undesirability all the time. i am aware that the fat on my body, the fat of my body, repulses some people who would otherwise be interested in me. my body puts me in a box that many do not want to open. partly this was by design. partly this was a test. would i want to sleep with me? if i met me? maybe. it's hard to say. maybe if i got to know me. the thing is, about this whole situation: i am married. i am not celibate. but there's an itch, still. a band-aid to be ripped off. another layer to strip away before i am truly swimming naked. before the moonlight and my ass make their fine acquaintance.

A TOUR OF YOUR MOTHER'S GARDEN

when your mother, who you remember
carrying an epi-pen in your early childhood
because she was allergic to bees and who
kept those epi-pens specifically
in the cool darkness of the towel closet
at the top of the stairs, last weekend
on your visit during the tour of her garden,
denied having ever been allergic to bees, said
you must have me confused with someone else—
some other mother perhaps, some
other version of a family—and next morning
showed you the fresh red welt on the hill
of her palm and said to you *see, i am
not allergic!* did you then picture a small fuzzy
body, your mother kneeling before a bed
of flowers, reaching out through static

my therapist said   you can't see gravity
being a parent   you can't taste outer space
is forever   cold-knuckled
anxious   day dreams

my ex said   i shouldn't leave my house
i was selfish   to die in a car crash
to refuse to   think of all the ways it could happen
have a baby   heart failure   blood clot   gas leak

my mother said   so many catastrophes
don't bother   the meteor could strike tonight
it's too much   while i sleep
for you   i want to stay

my husband   i wouldn't know
said   i couldn't stop it
i want   to hush these thoughts
what you want   would be so restful

not-child   in the future
you were wanted &   i am dead   with
so   much more to do
what   next

WHY I WON'T BE YOUR MOTHER

not born but extruded.
magmabelly. the pressure of your arrival
bulging my nail beds. throw back my head
and push. there you'd be: lava eruption
from my mouth. bubblemelt ejection
running down my chin. your first cry
steam whistling between my teeth.
i'd gather you. scoop you fiery from ceiling.
the nest between my breasts.
streaking down my legs. living rock
piling at my ankles.
i would form the molten of you.
my volcanic baby. my not existing child.
your body so different from my body. but of it.
i'd hold you. i'd name you. red pulsing.
never cooling. in a chamber
gradually filling up with ash.

I THOUGHT YOU WERE GIVING ME FLOWERS

you are a lightly supervised child
planted directly in the path to my table.

you reach out. i think you are
handing me the bluets in your fist.

you're not. you're prodding
my belly and demanding "what's that."

look kid, life comes at you fast.
right now you're just bothering a stranger

while your mom samples local oysters,
but soon enough you'll be lamenting

dad-bod and your receding hairline.
so i hope you grow up strong, with self-respect.

someday you might meet somebody wonderful.
not perfect.

at the end of your time together,
you could even tell your girlfriend

your true opinion of her body,
and leave her

for the last time. take the 1am train
to your parents' house where you can start again.

she might become a poet
in the wake of your departure,

try a dozen times to write
the weight of your word: *disgust.*

every attempt a molded-plastic failure.
none of this is certain.

when i meet your toddler incarnation
at a restaurant several states away,

i scribble about it
because of habit. i know you are not you.

i know you are a child
exploring the world with your hands.

forgive this dry husk of anger.
my grumbling seedpods.

rustling. a dandelion's wisp.

THE PHONE SEX POEM

i don't really know what i want.
and i do.
i mostly do not like what it is that i want.
it is mostly counterproductive to my happiness.

i have a better idea of what i like, and what i don't.
sometimes i even know why.
what put me on that path.
what has gotten in my way.

i try not to conflate the concept of dicks
with the concept of men with the concept of sex.
but often when i think about sex
i think about the dicks i have learned to navigate

like spokes on the steering wheel
of a big old-timey sailing ship.
only it's a dick wheel. wheel of dick.
that's my new game show.

once when i was fucked up on benzos
i called an acquaintance
and asked to give him a blowjob
so i could "stay practiced in the artform."
my heart wasn't in it though
and halfway through i gave up,
ashamed of every time i ever made myself
a dirty rag.

this is what i don't want:
to become a desperate mouth.

i would like to be 22 again.
22 seems like a good time to be having sex,
a golden age for test-tubing experiences.

when i was 22, i was still 17.
when i was 17, i was 13,
and fearful.

my whole life i misunderstood
the importance of play.

MORE MOM FACTS

The wallpaper in my mother's guest room soothes,
fuzzy to the touch. My mother's shampoo
suds well and smells expensive.

My mother reads me passages from her old journal
while we sit in her garden in the sun.

When she was 15, my mother was sent abroad
to study French. My mother sassed Madame
and belched at Pierre. My mother never forgets

I can't walk far or fast while we travel to the cinema
to see a matinee. Afterwards, we compare notes.

Our opinions are the same opinions. Our noses
are the same pink noses. My mother is a mother.
I am nobody's mother. Sometimes I feel a little

like my mother's daughter. I've been cared for.
I feel like I'm fifteen again, belching at the table.

BEFORE YOUR NAME

1

All I do is get old in rooms. A room so tall that trees
never brush the ceiling. A bus running from room
to room, always late. Sometimes my whole house
floats into the sky. The doors to my house
never lock. Anybody can just walk right in,
but I can't leave. I'm having a sleepover party.
All my friends are here. Gonna watch a movie.
Gonna have an orgy or lay the table for a feast
from whatever's in the fridge. I lived my whole life
doing whatever, and then I heard about you. Heard you
were on your way. I love that about you. Welcome.

2

All I do is old. Trees
never run late. My house,
the sky. Anybody can leave.
All my friends from my whole life
and you. I love you.

3

All I do is love you.

I BET I'M GOING TO COMPLETE MY LIFE-CYCLE AT A DENNY'S

the way salmon go upstream to spawn.
I'll slump onto my half-devoured Grand Slamwich,
be gradually absorbed into the Denny's ecosystem.

Fact: a whale fall like me would sustain
the area theatre kids for weeks.
The first time I hold a baby I am already 36.

She is only two weeks old with a scrunchy face
and mealworm fingers. Little arms conducting
an orchestra of nobody. I decide I am to be Ant Cat—

not the fussier Aunt Catherine.
In the car later, I fight my knuckle of tears.
I'm making notes for this poem in a document

originally used to plan for a takeout order:
Sesame chicken. Hot and sour soup. Large pork fried rice.
Crab rangoons. I traded my motherness for a lifetime

of restaurant food. Why's it so hard to keep choosing
my life? Maybe eventually I'll get used to holding
other people's babies. But I have this. I have you.

INHERITANCE

every poet has at least one poem called *inheritance*
and mine is about the rogue porno i found lurking
among my dead grandmother's DVD collection.
i kept it. obviously. i put it in my pile and quietly took it
home to examine further. now, i check the release date
on the back. 2006. the DVD itself has been gently scuffed.
all evidence suggesting it's Been Watched Before.
i'm performing forensics on Playboy's Nude Dorm Party.
on the front of the cardboard sleeve is a lady
covering her nipples with her hands. inside is a lady
with her tits all the way out. hark: a scene index.
the lady with her tits out is also somehow wearing
a crochet sweater. i have recently taken up crochet.
it's been making me feel closer to my grandmother,
a crafty woman. a woman whose husband had,
before his death, a subscription to Playboy Magazine.
i mean, it all makes sense. the existence of this porno
in my grandma's belongings is perfectly explicable.
i still barked a despairing whoop when first i saw it
cuddled up between Ratatouille and the Minions movie.
i wanted it to be hers. wanted porn to be something
we had in common. a softcore tragedy. tits casserole
at thanksgiving dinner. i'm sad. what if i framed it.
what if i set it on the mantelpiece in a place of honor,
told you stories about how giving my grandmother was,
how i don't ever once remember her complaining about shit
my grandpa did and didn't do. i want to remember her
with joy. i want to remember her with pleasure. i say
it's grandma's porno now. i hope she wouldn't be ashamed.
i'm laughing with sorrow souping up my lungs.
i wonder what she wanted. if i could ask, i wouldn't.

NOTES & ACKNOWLEDGMENTS

The title of *Money Changes Everything* is borrowed from a song title of a Cyndi Lauper song, from the 1983 album She's So Unusual.

The poem *Sucking and Fucking* is after Billy Collins, but please nobody tell that to him.

In the Viral Video is a pantoum.

The poem *Intrusive Thinking* is a contrapuntal.

The full text of *Dissociative Episode as Gaussian Blur* is: i could admit i never liked him / then came the bad conversation / podcasts and photoshop painting / coffee all day long to stay upright / time must still be passing but / i've been elsewhere for four days / the snow falls on indifferent pines / my reflection in the window again / throw brick through a television / where does the anger go anyway / i wish i could just put it down

Ekphrasis of "BOWLING ALLEY GANGBANG - Bukaki [sic] Ending" references two other poems: Good Bones by Maggie Smith, and The Two-Headed Calf by Laura Gilpin.

Thank you to the publications which first published these poems:

DIAGRAM, Dissociative Episode as Gaussian Blur

Drunk in a Midnight Choir, How to Like It

Fauxmoir, Cutting Cards

Okay Donkey, Bundle of Joy

Passengers Journal, interitance, Ekphrasis of Bowling Alley Gangbang

GRATITUDES

Niko Letendre-Cahillane • Zeke Russell • Maya Williams • Myles Taylor • Ally Ang • Josh Savory • MJ Majpiedi • Giovanna Lomanto • Zoe-Aline Howard • Ilyus Evander • Anna Binkovitz • Lyd Havens • Jelal Huyler • Karan Sheldon • Megan McDermott • JL Roberts • Robbie Dunning • James Stenning-Barnes • Claudia Wilson

CATHERINE WEISS is a poet and artist from Maine, living in Western Massachusetts. They are the author of the Smash Mouth-inspired chapbook-length golden shovel *Fervor*, as well as pro-wrestling themed tête-bêche poetry chapbook *Winners & Losers*. Catherine's full-length poetry collections are titled *Wolf Girls vs. Horse Girls*, *Griefcake*, and *Big Money Porno Mommy*. Their work has appeared in numerous publications, including DIAGRAM, Tinderbox, Passengers Journal, Fugue, and Taco Bell Quarterly.